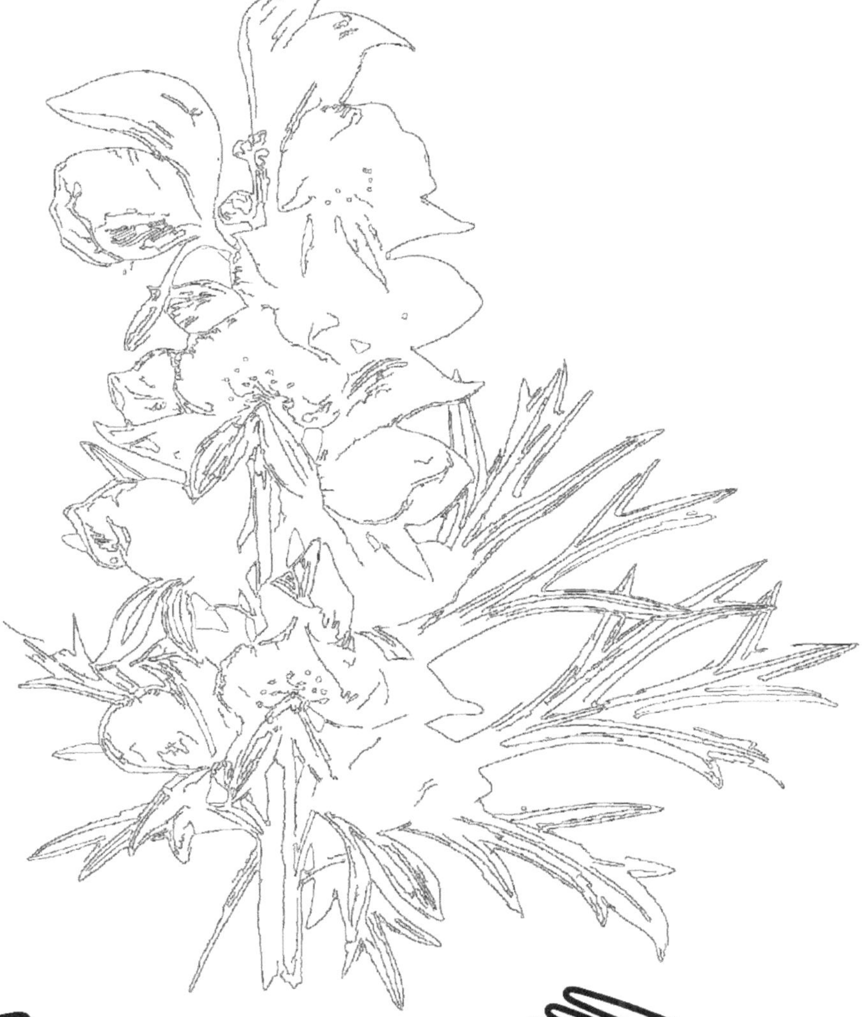

Enjoy Coloring!!!...

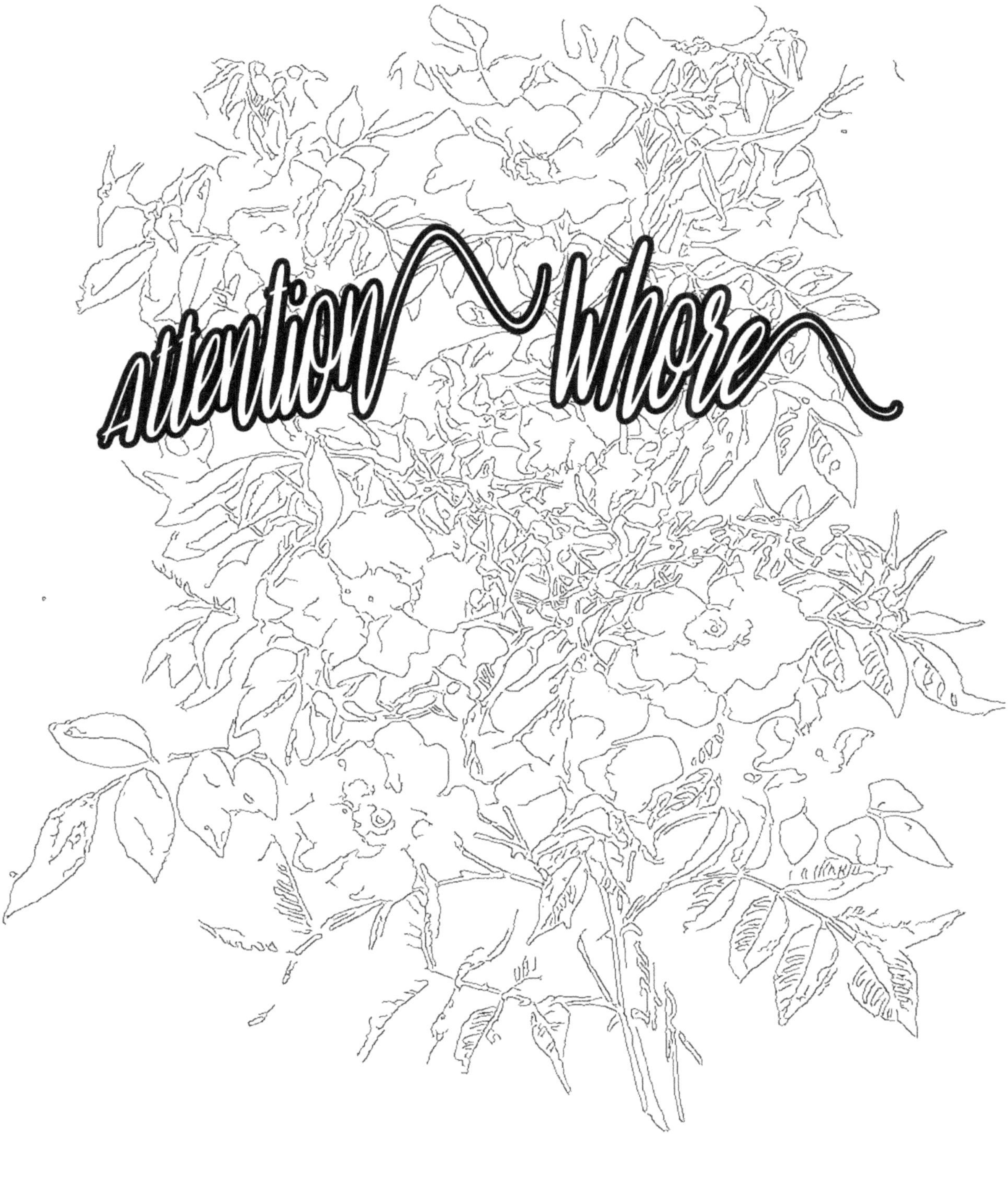
attention whore

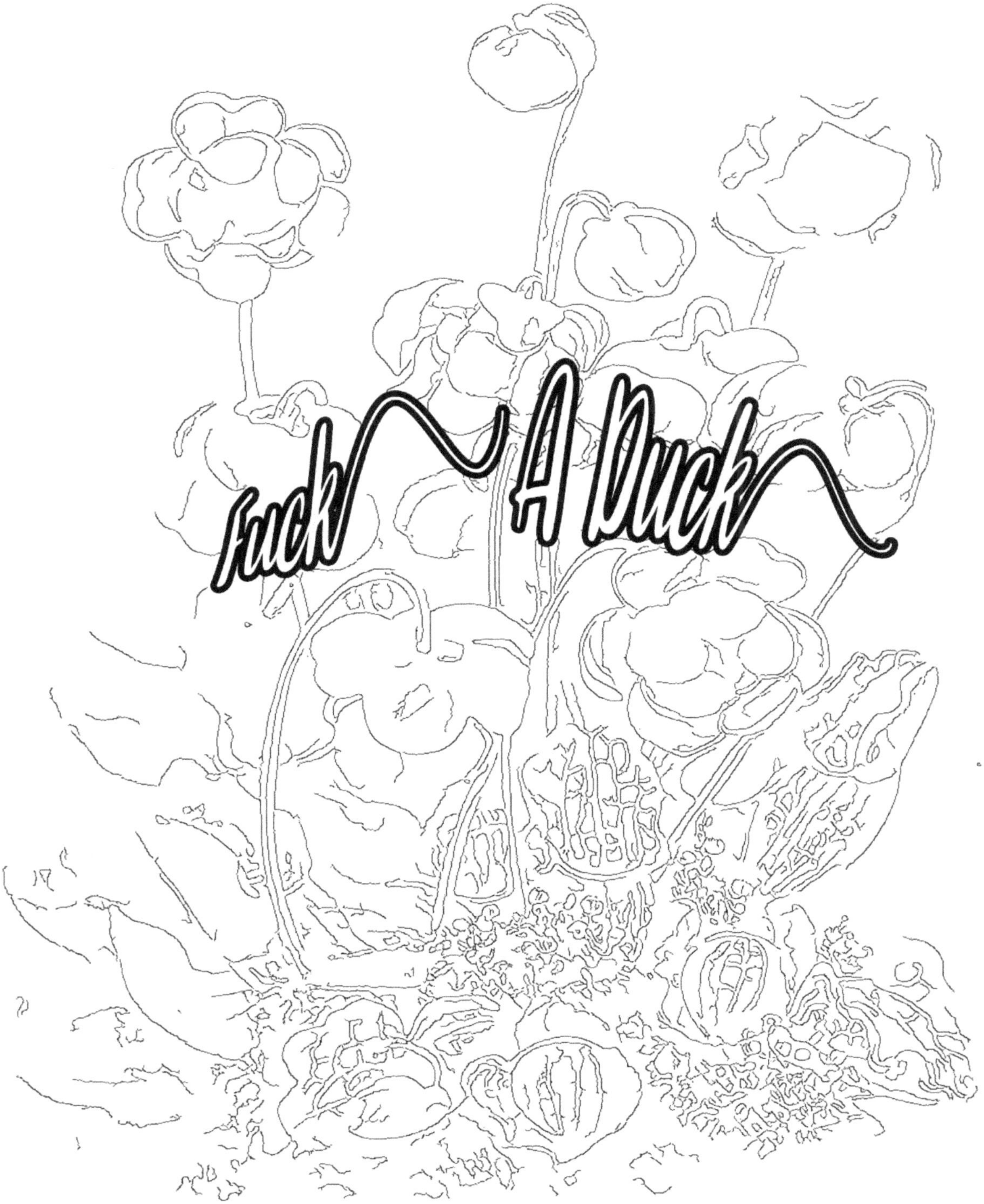
Fuck A Duck

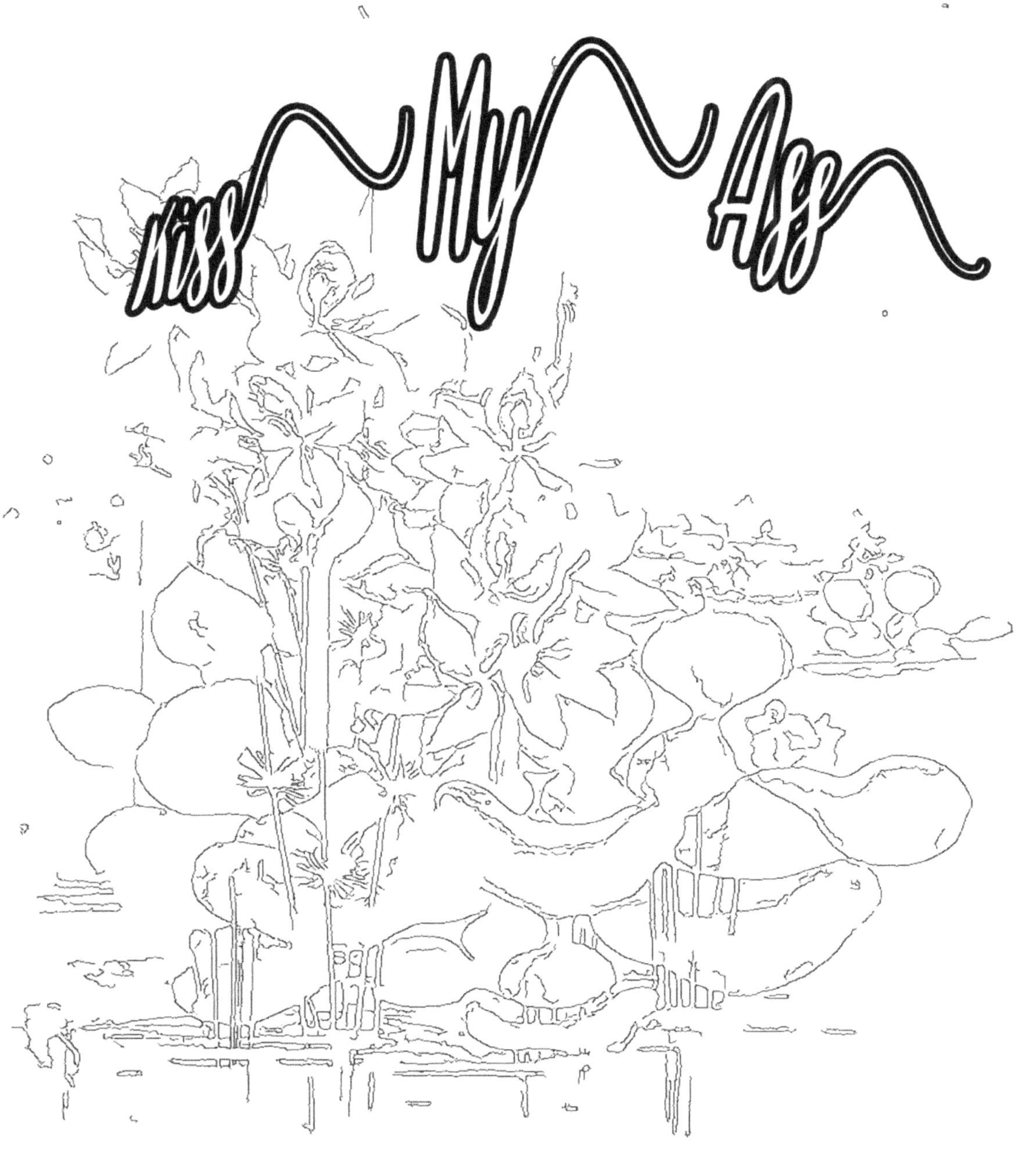
Kiss My Ass

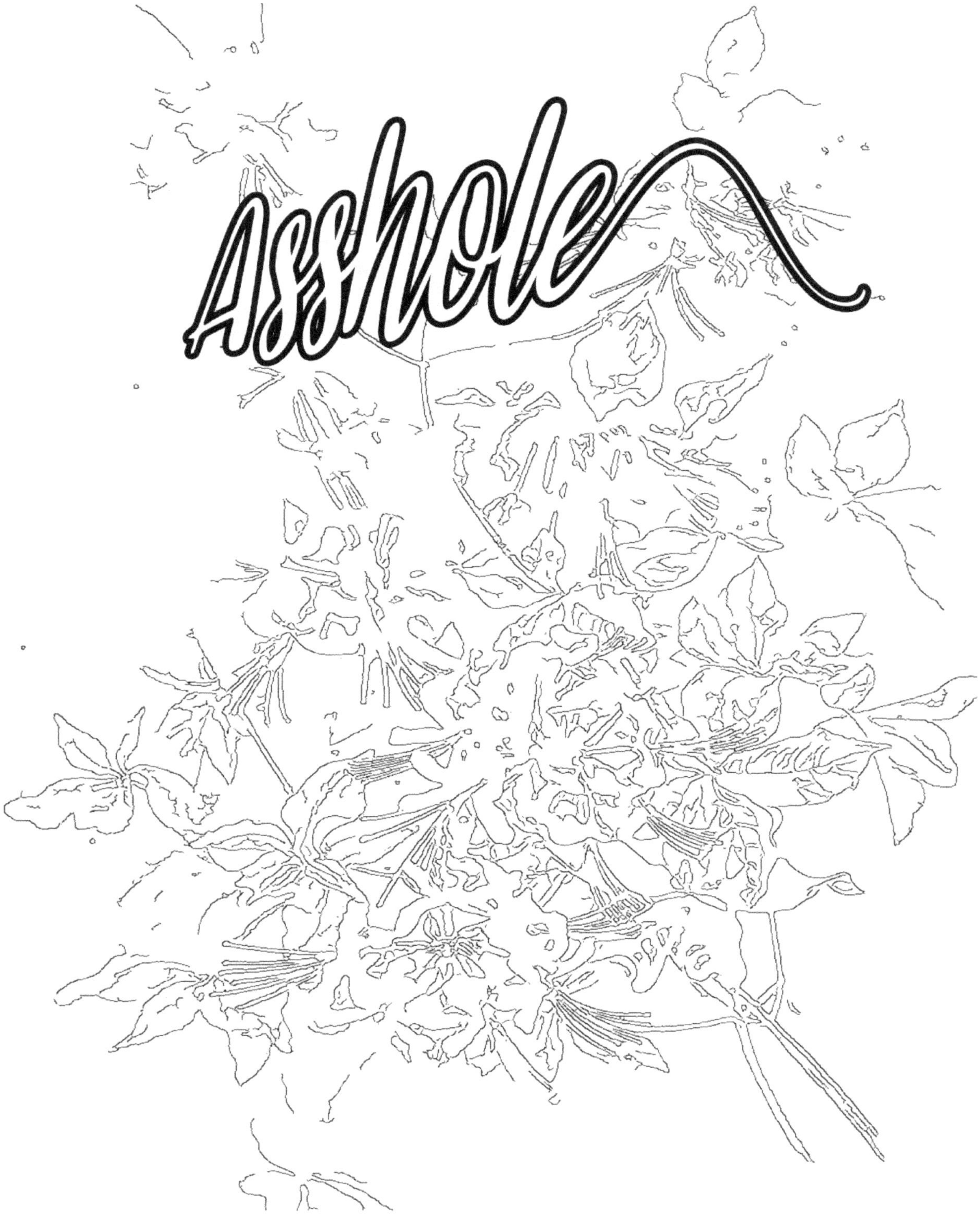
Asshole

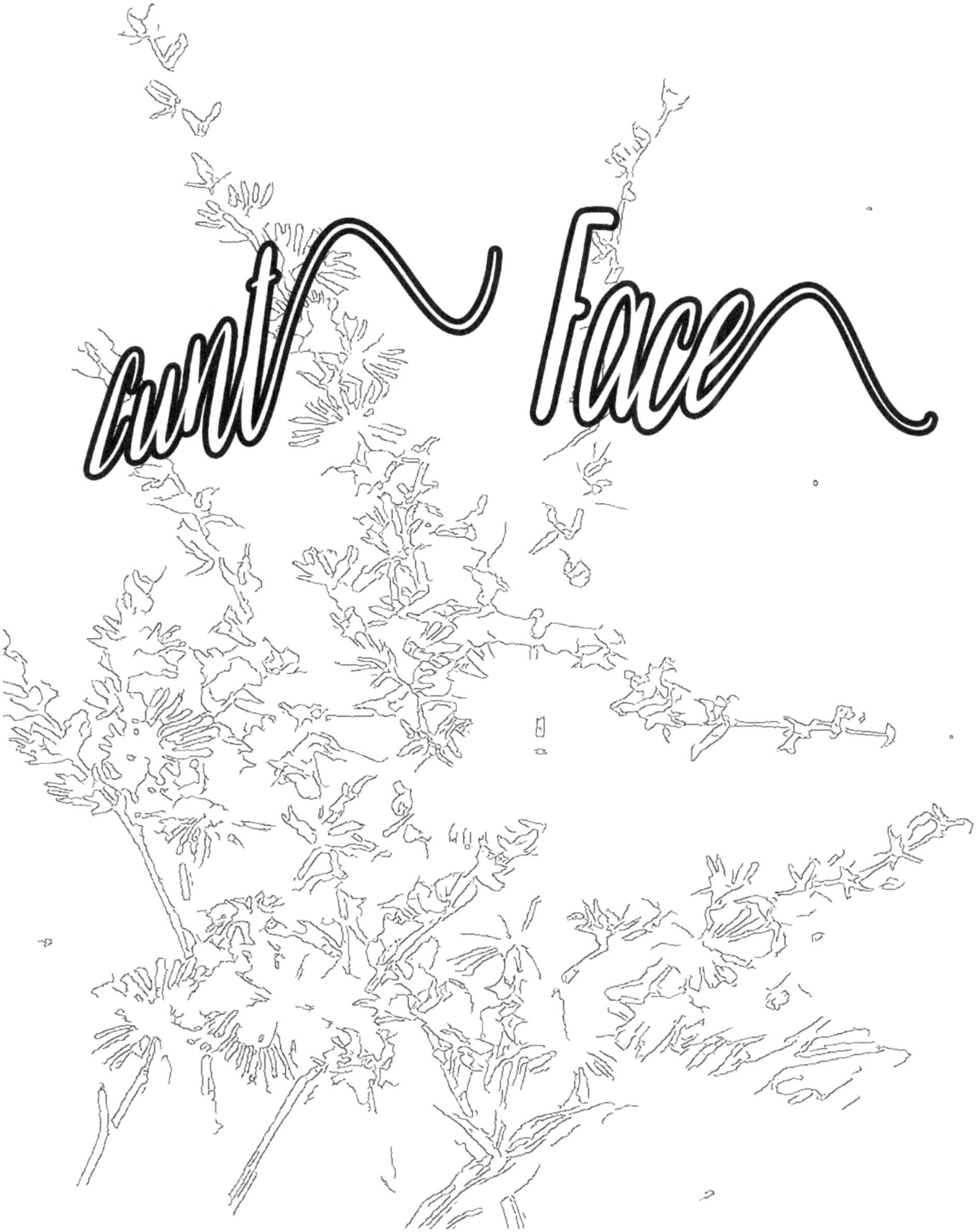
Cunt Face

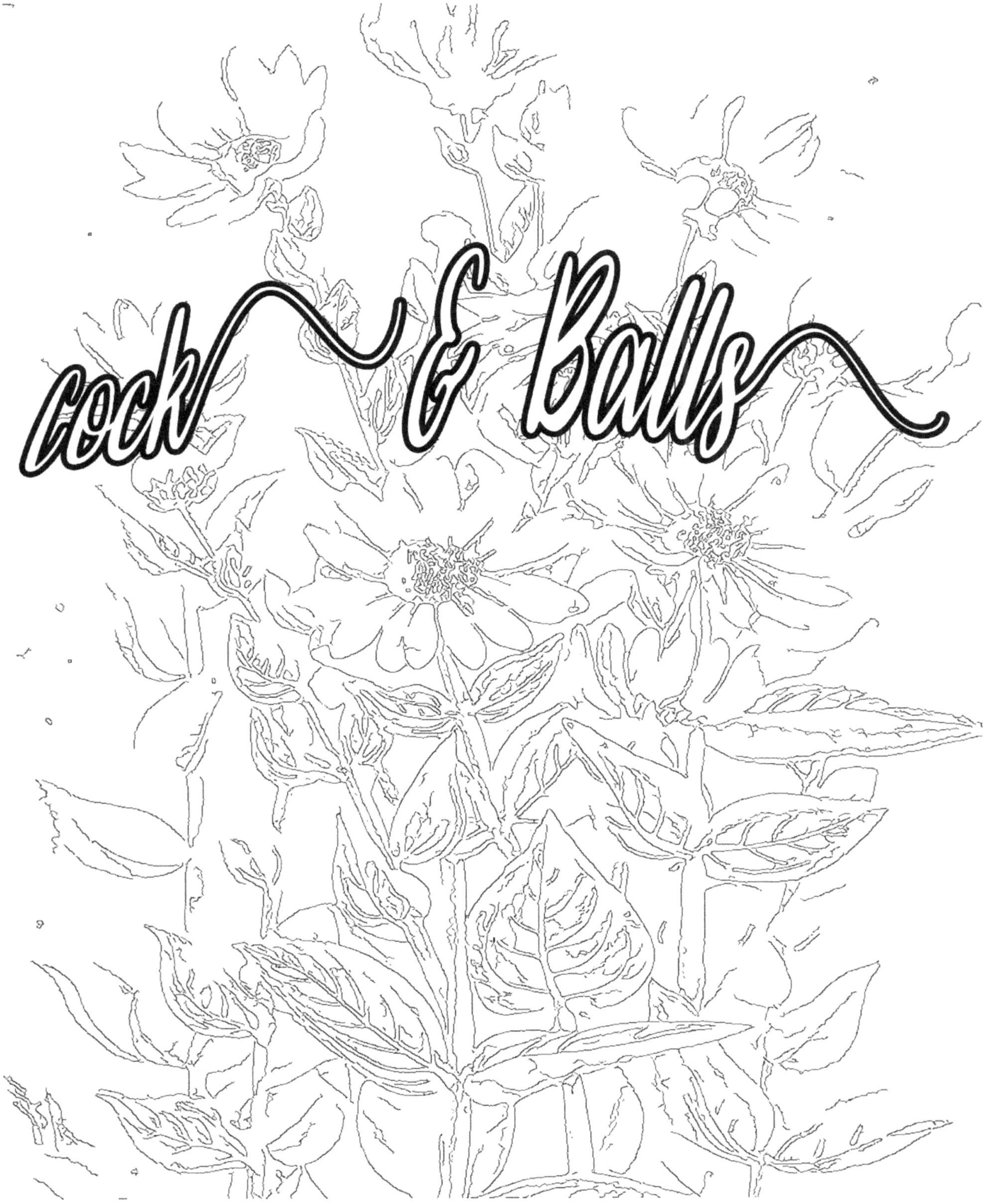
cock & Balls

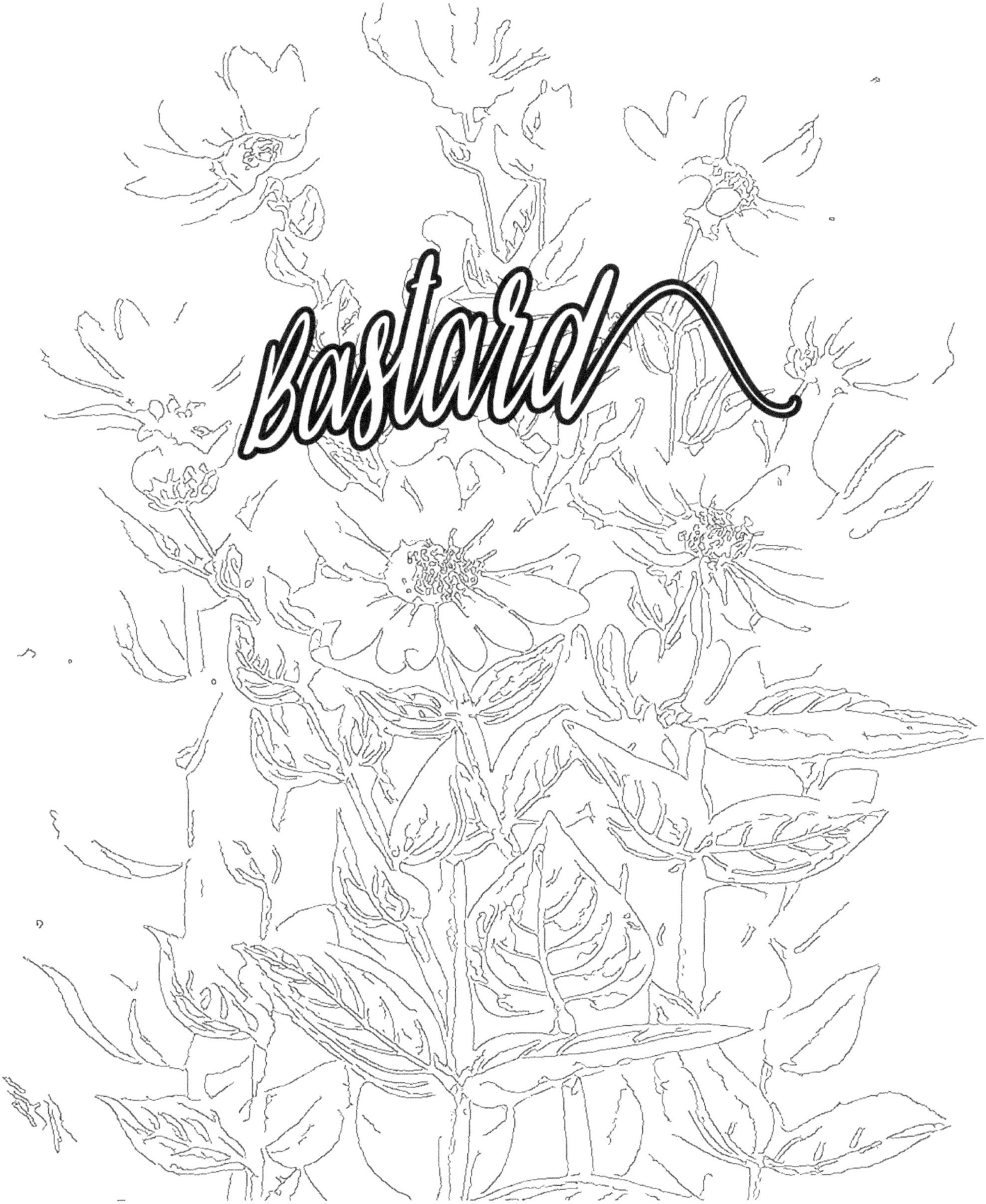
Bastard

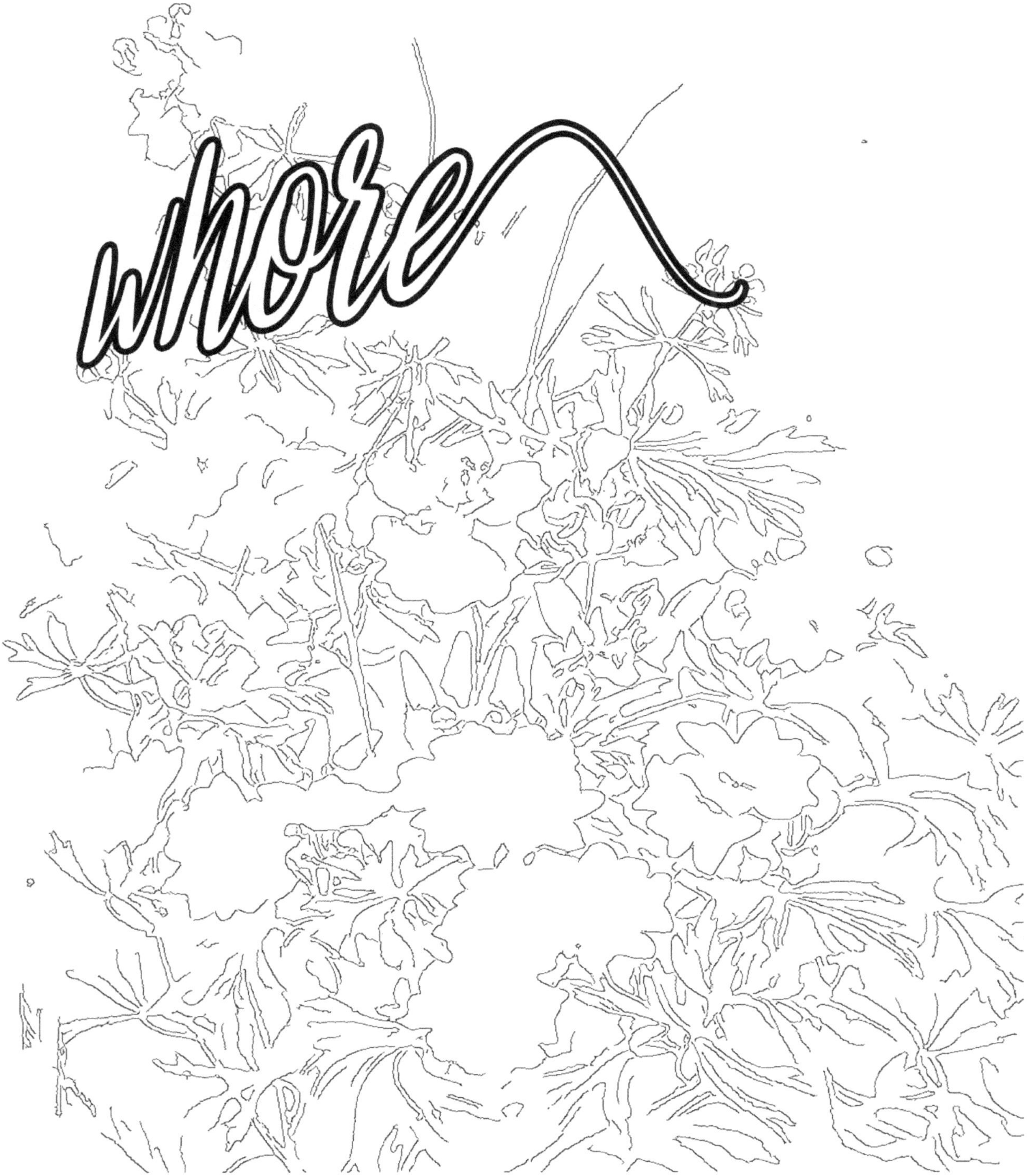
whore

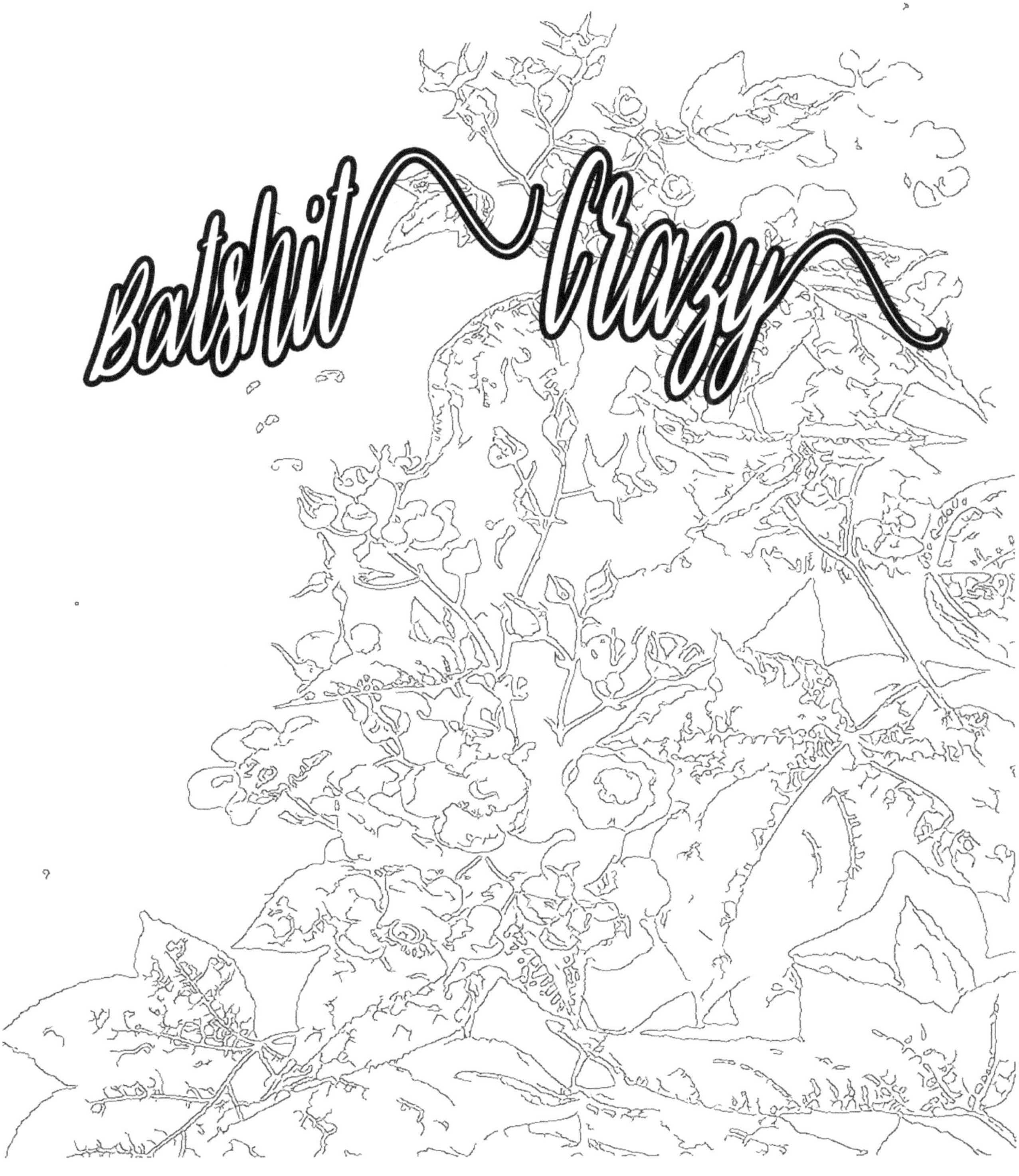
Batshit Crazy

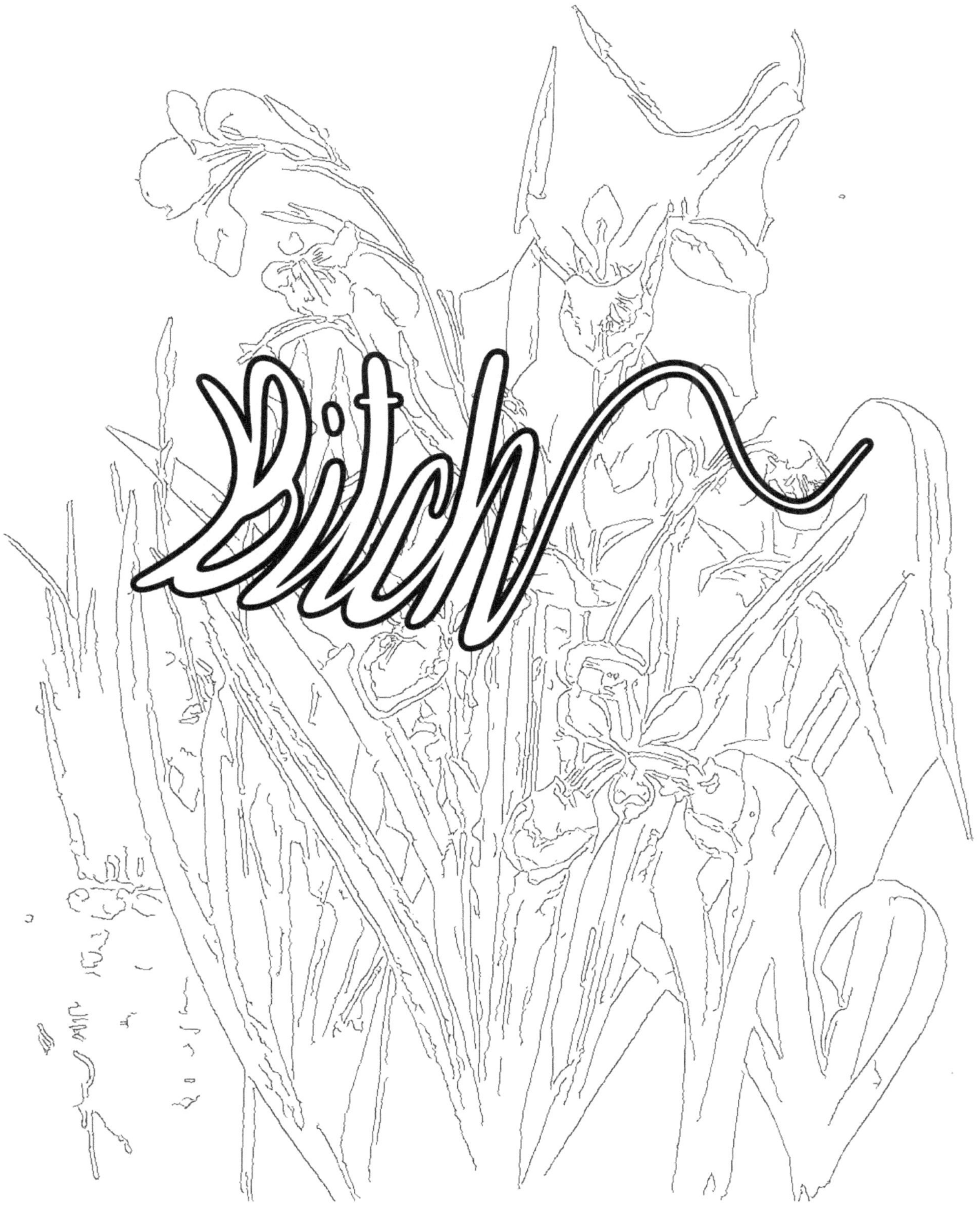
Bitch

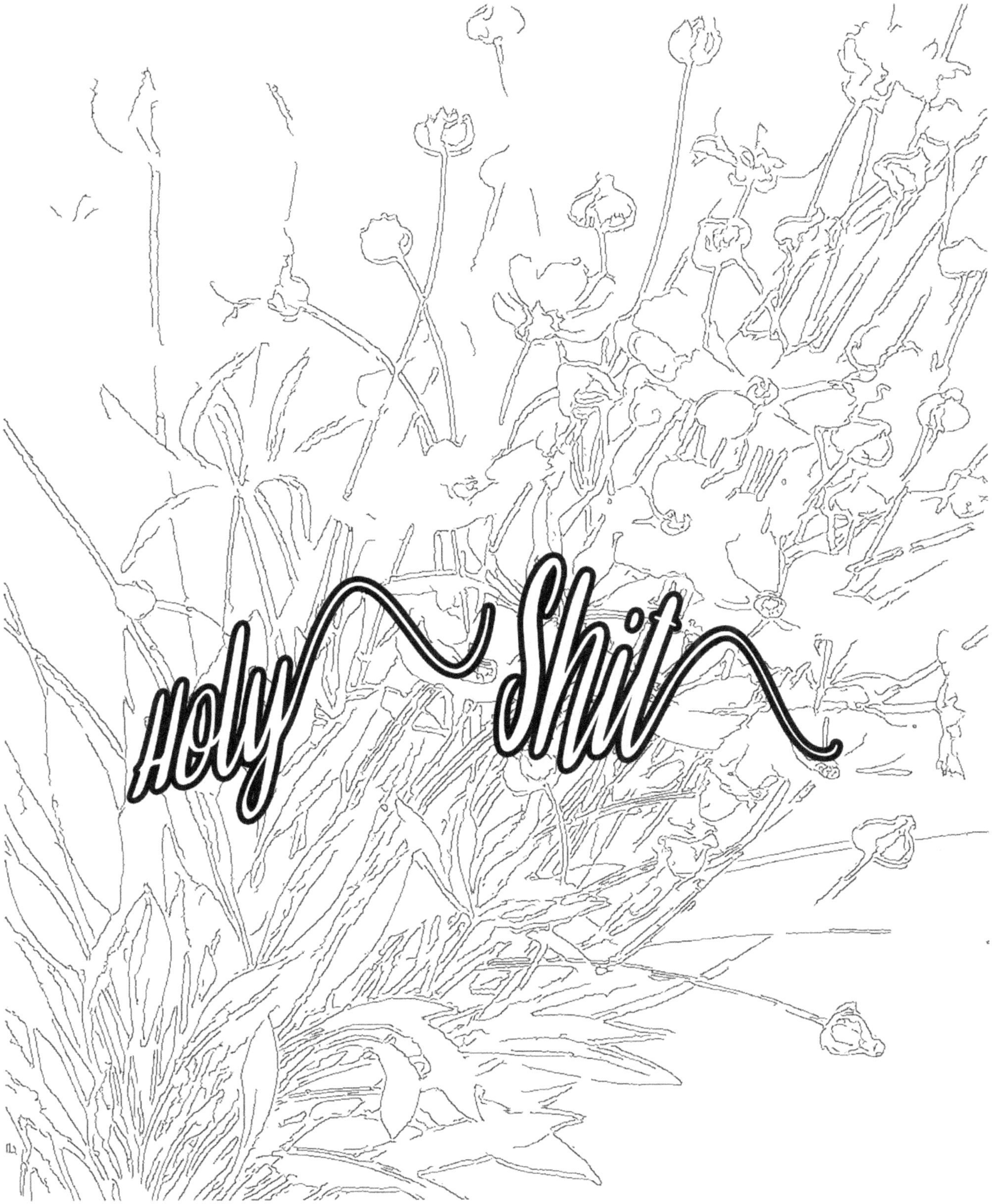
Holy Shit

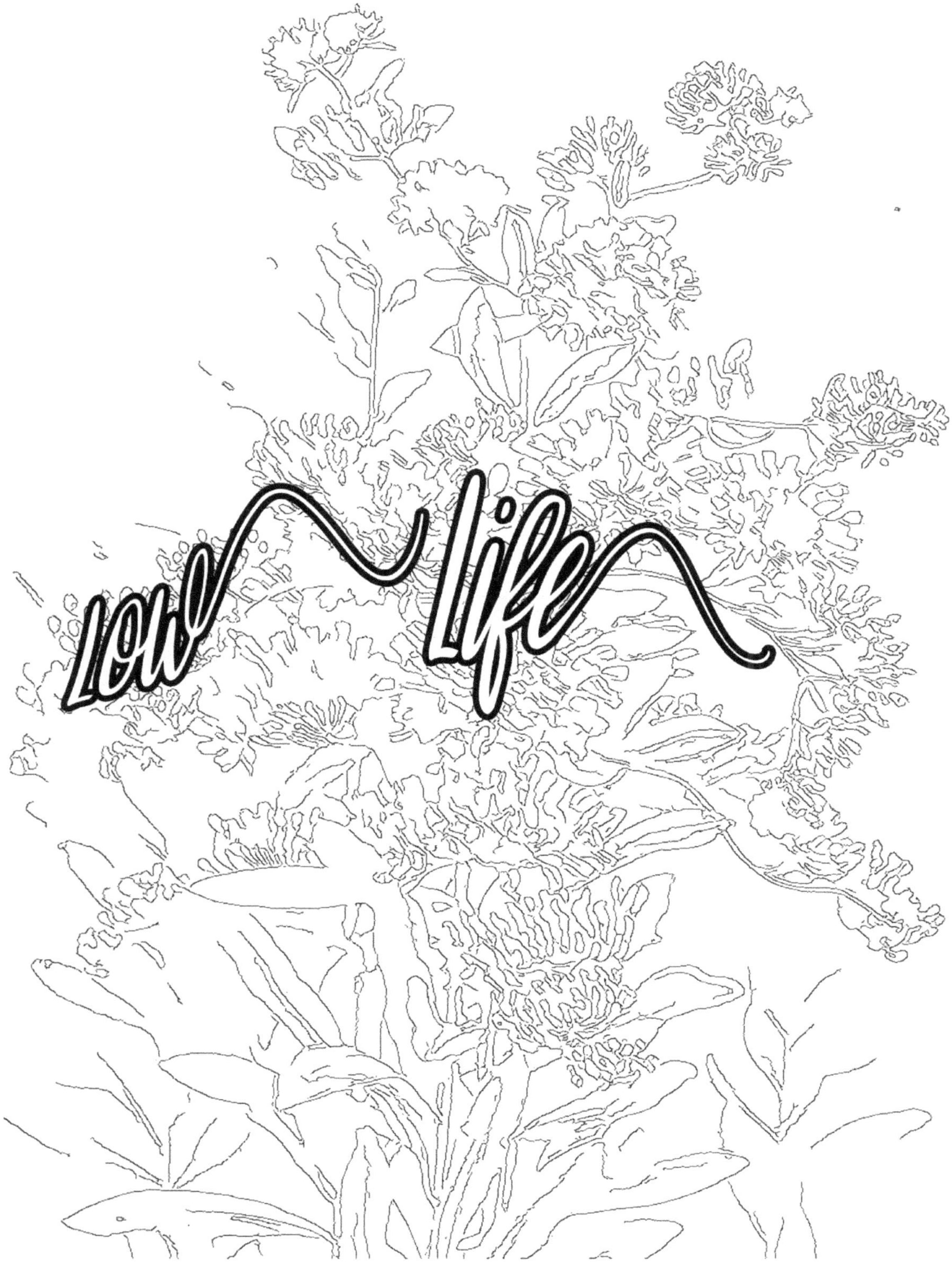
Low Life

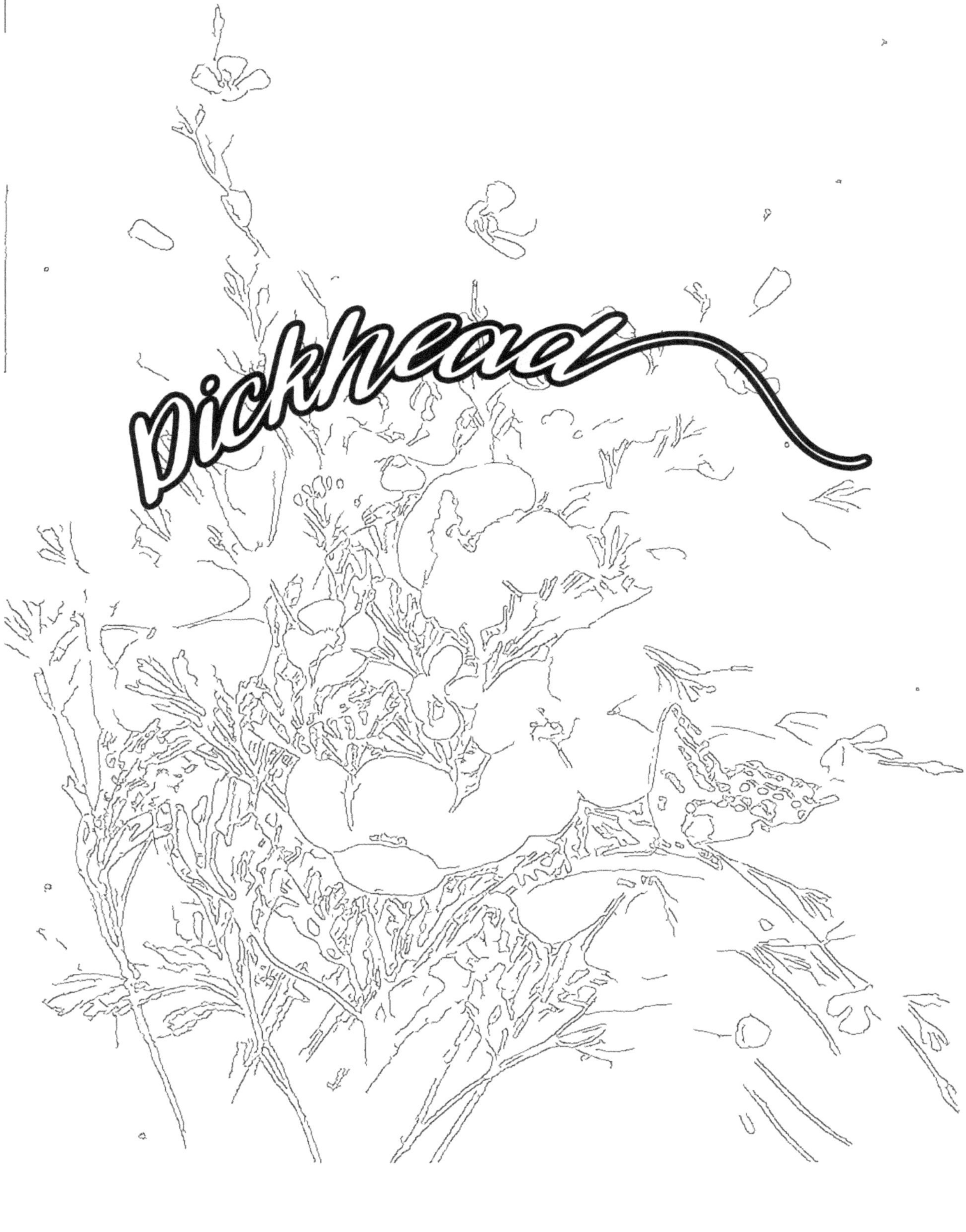
Dickhead

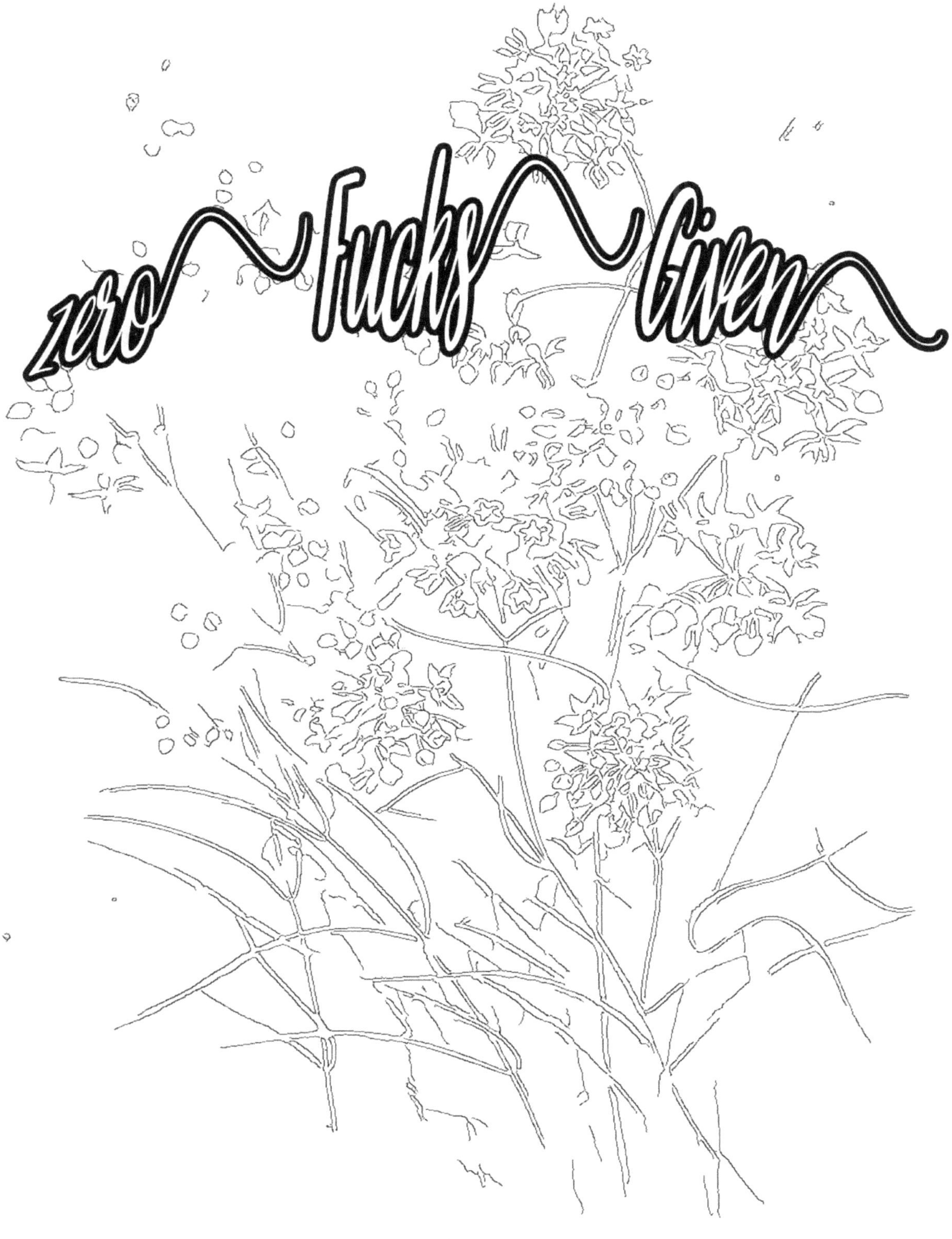
zero Fucks Given

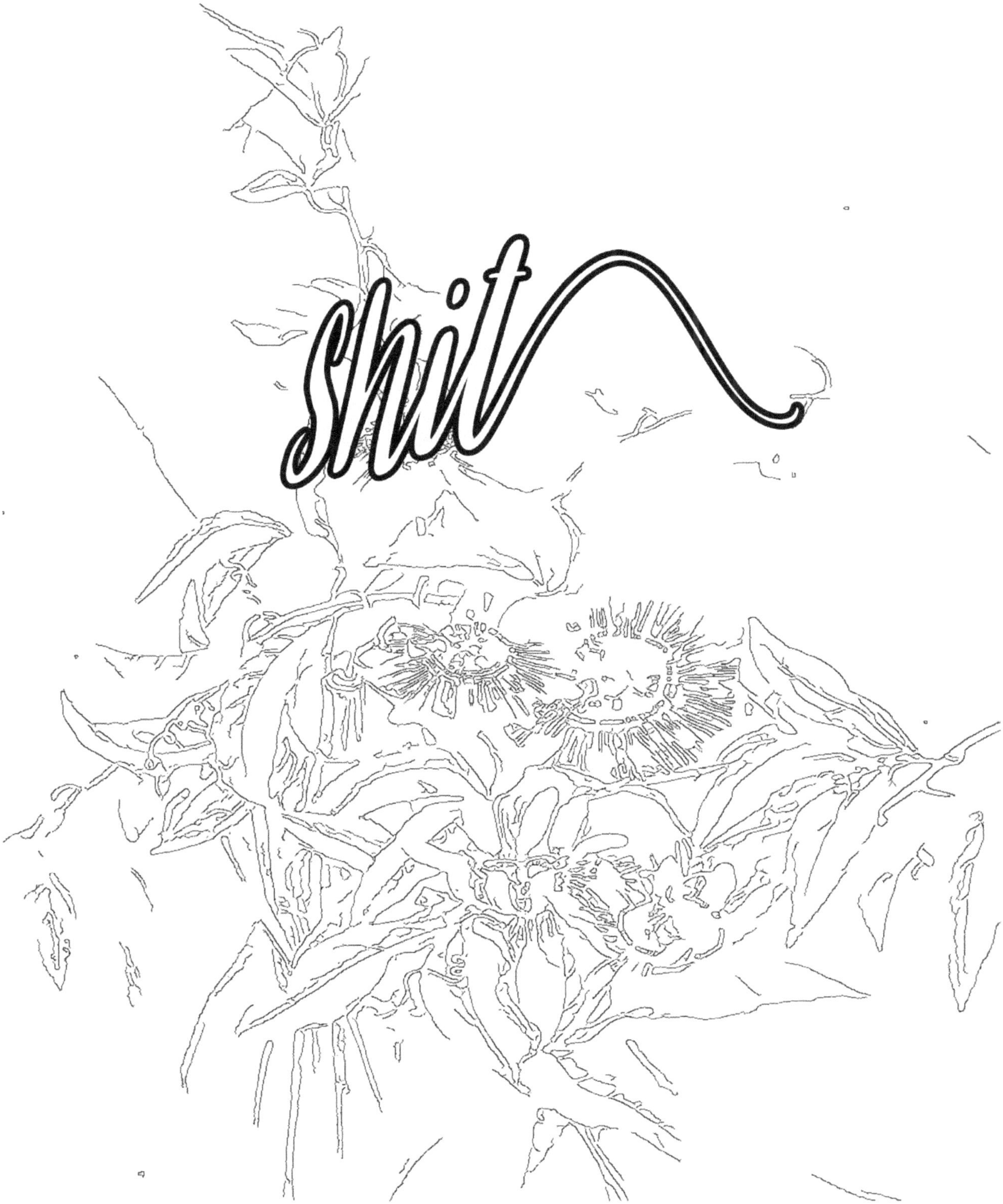
shit

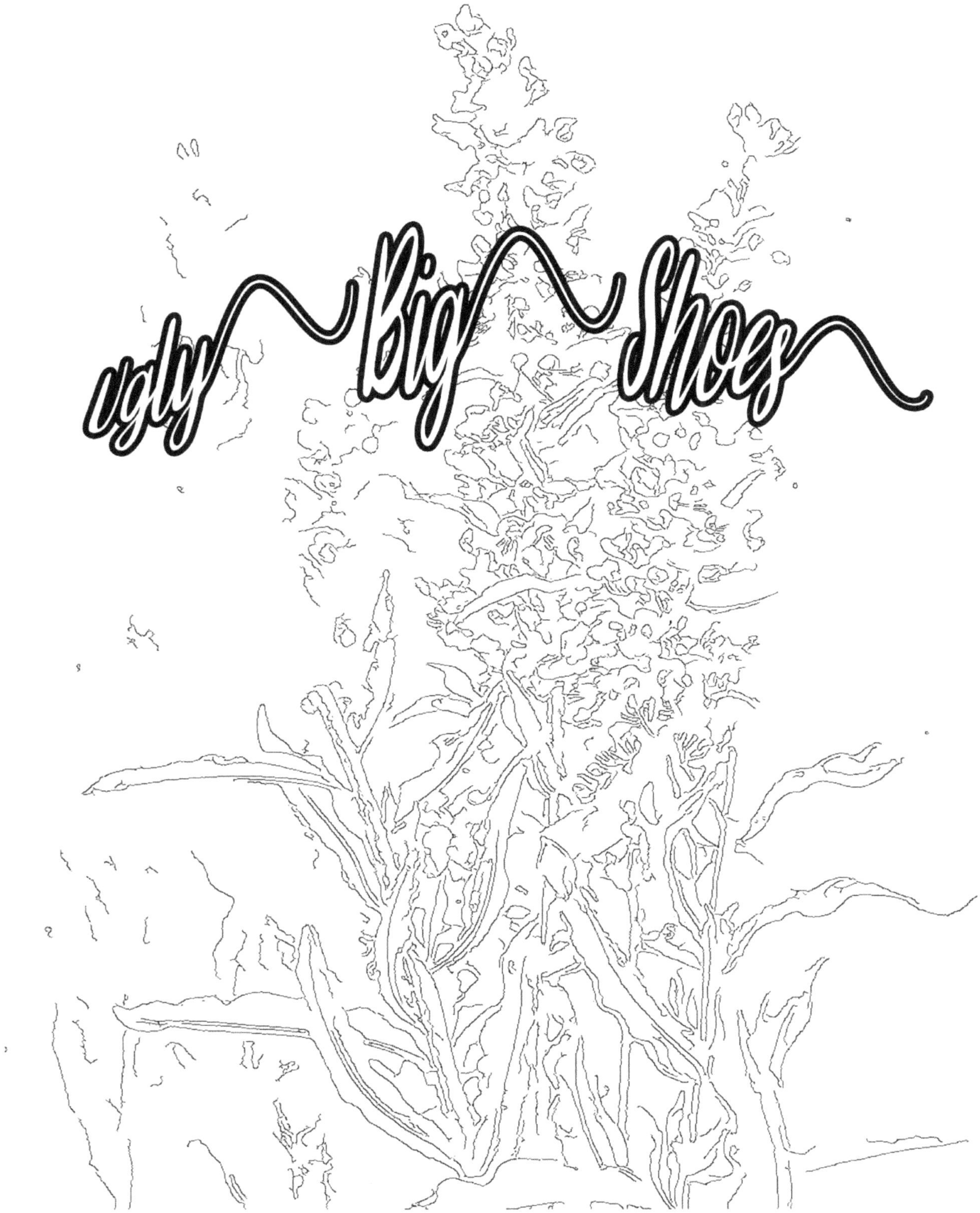
ugly Big Shoes

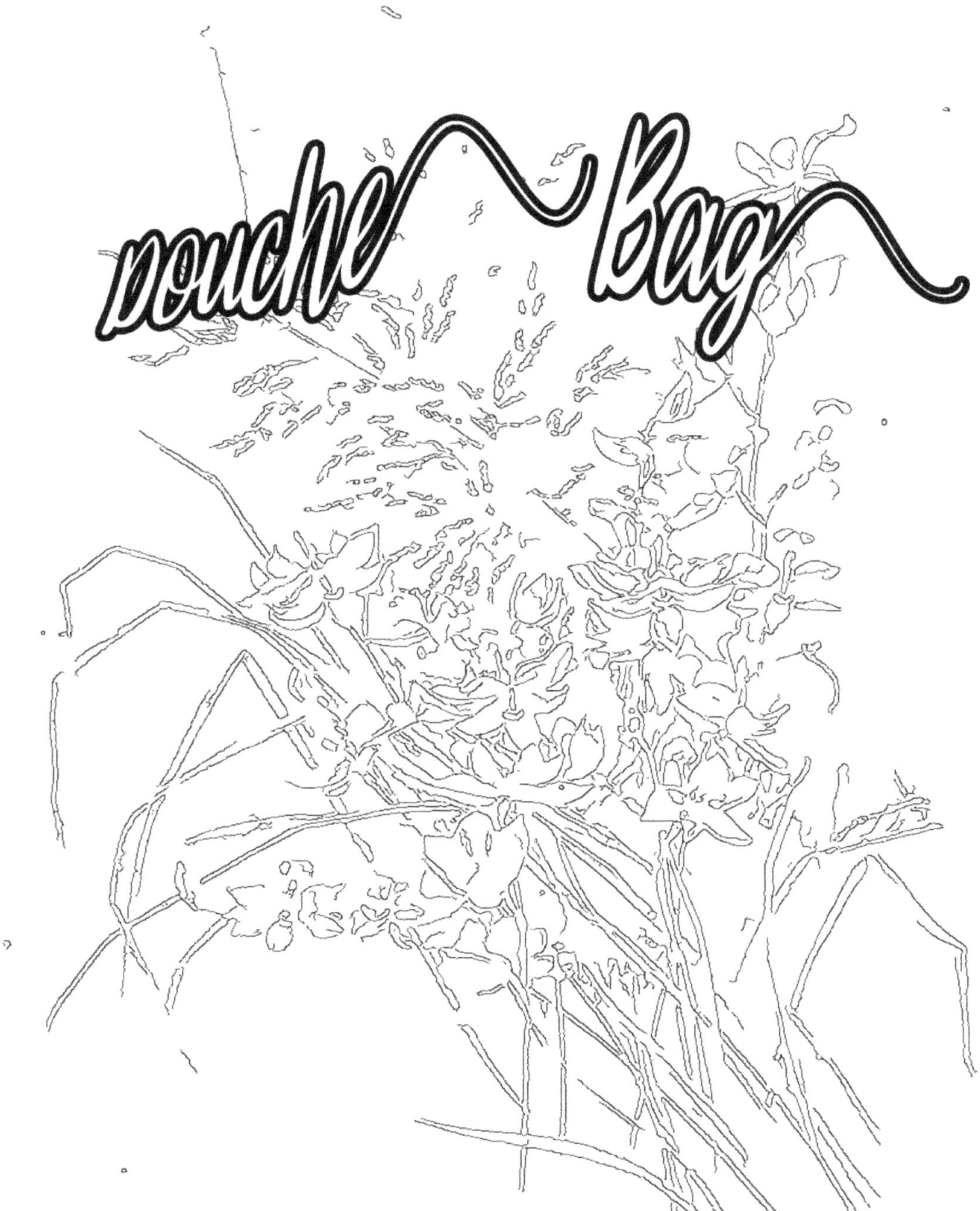
Douche Bag

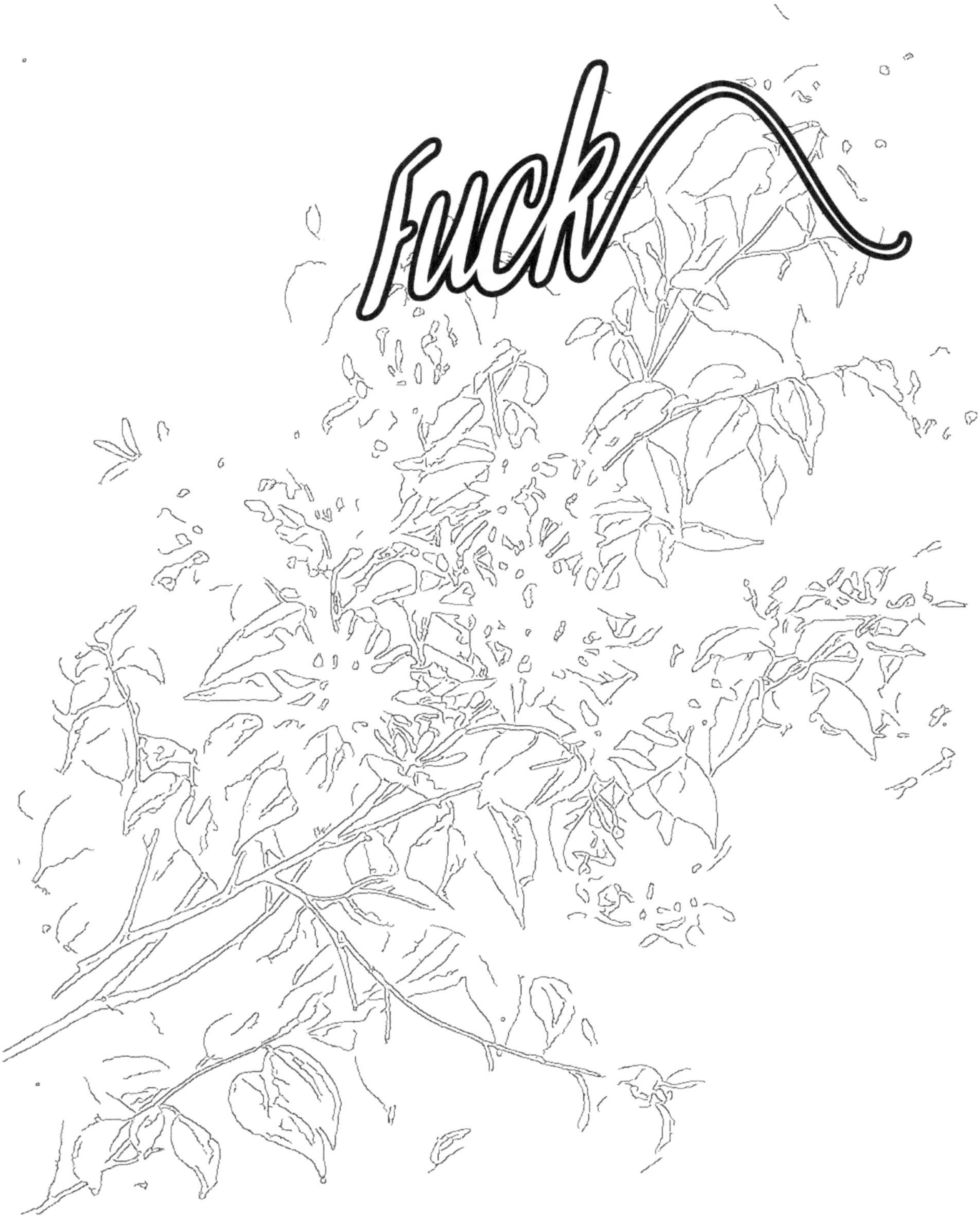
Fuck

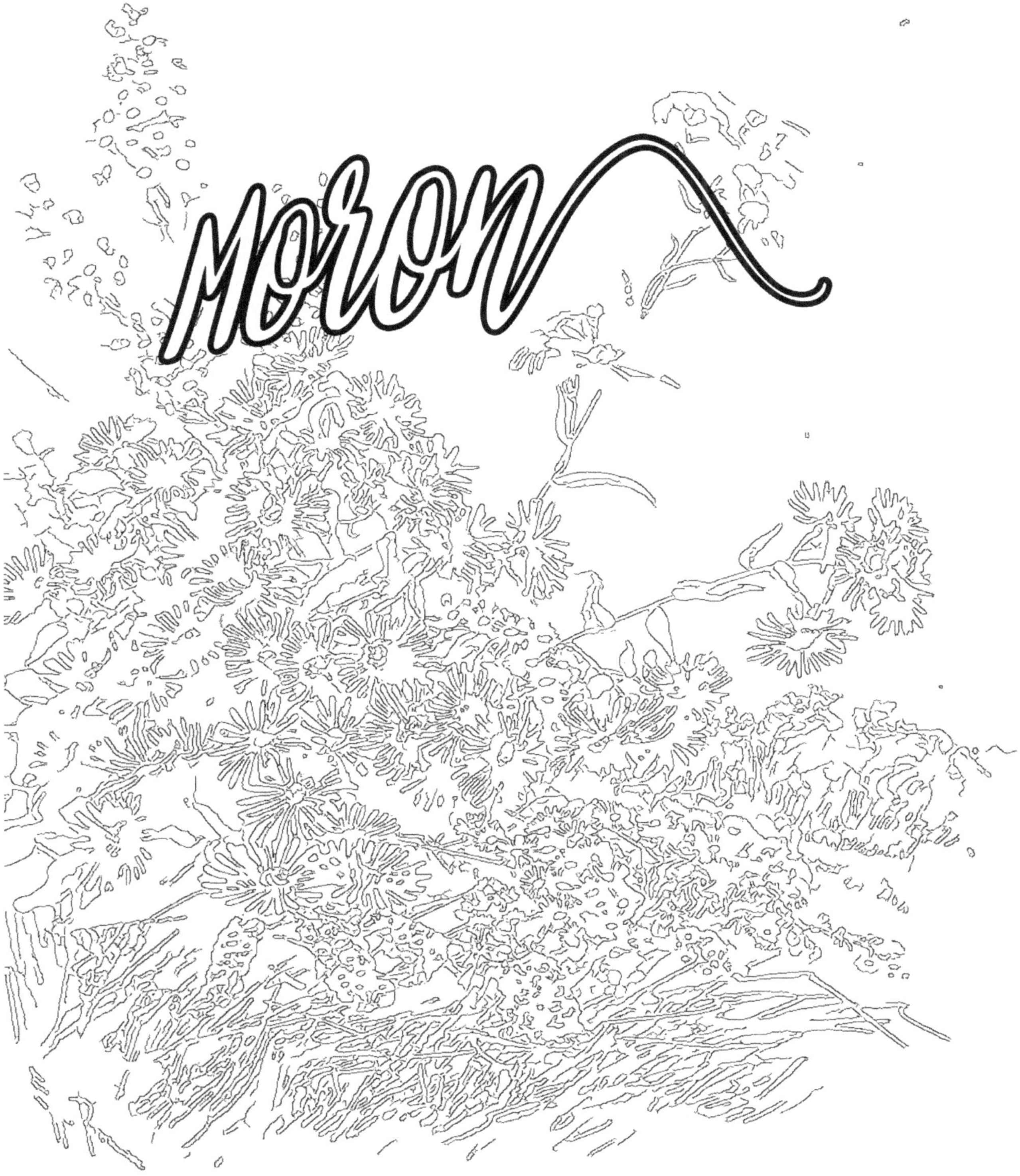
Moron

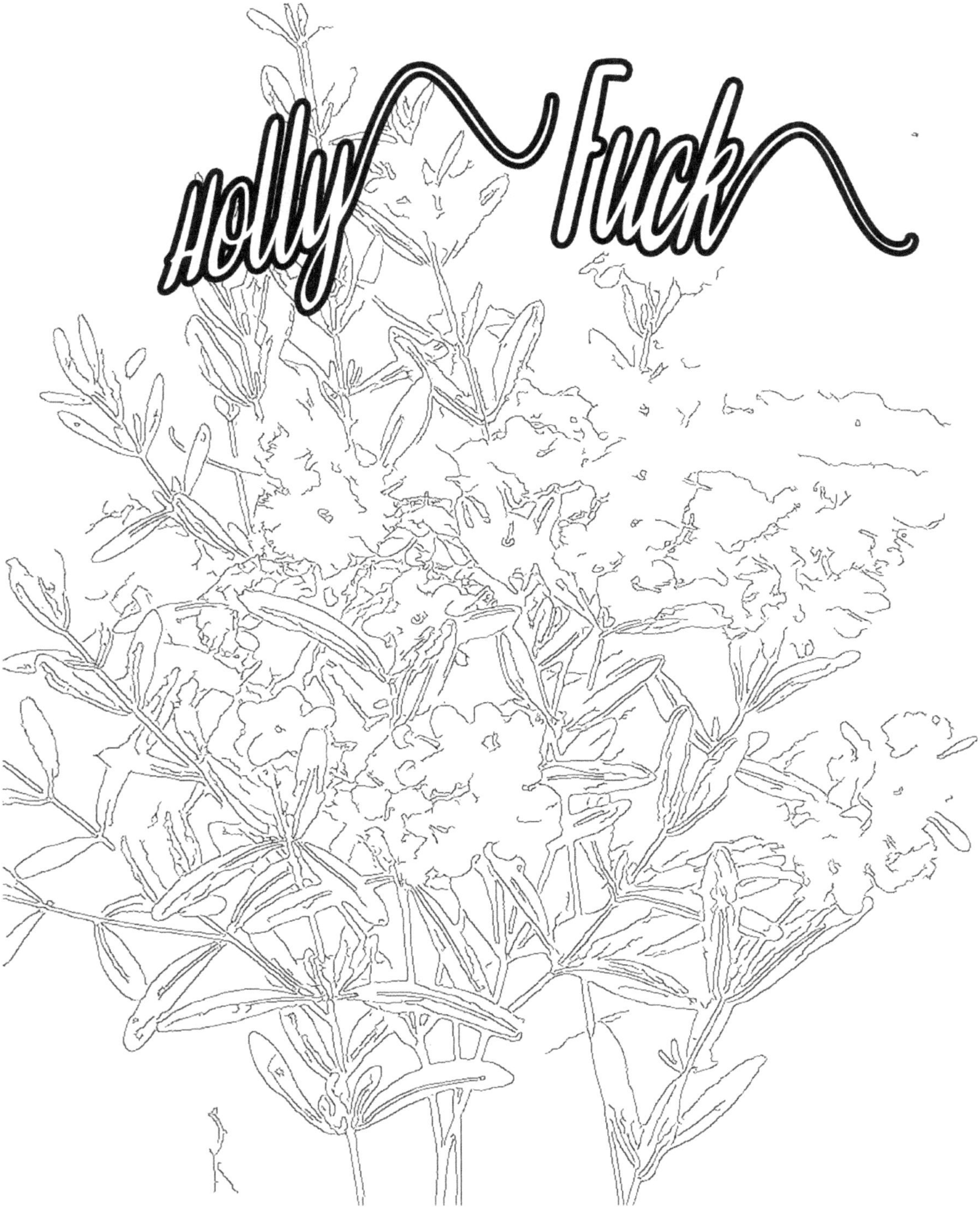
Holly Fuck

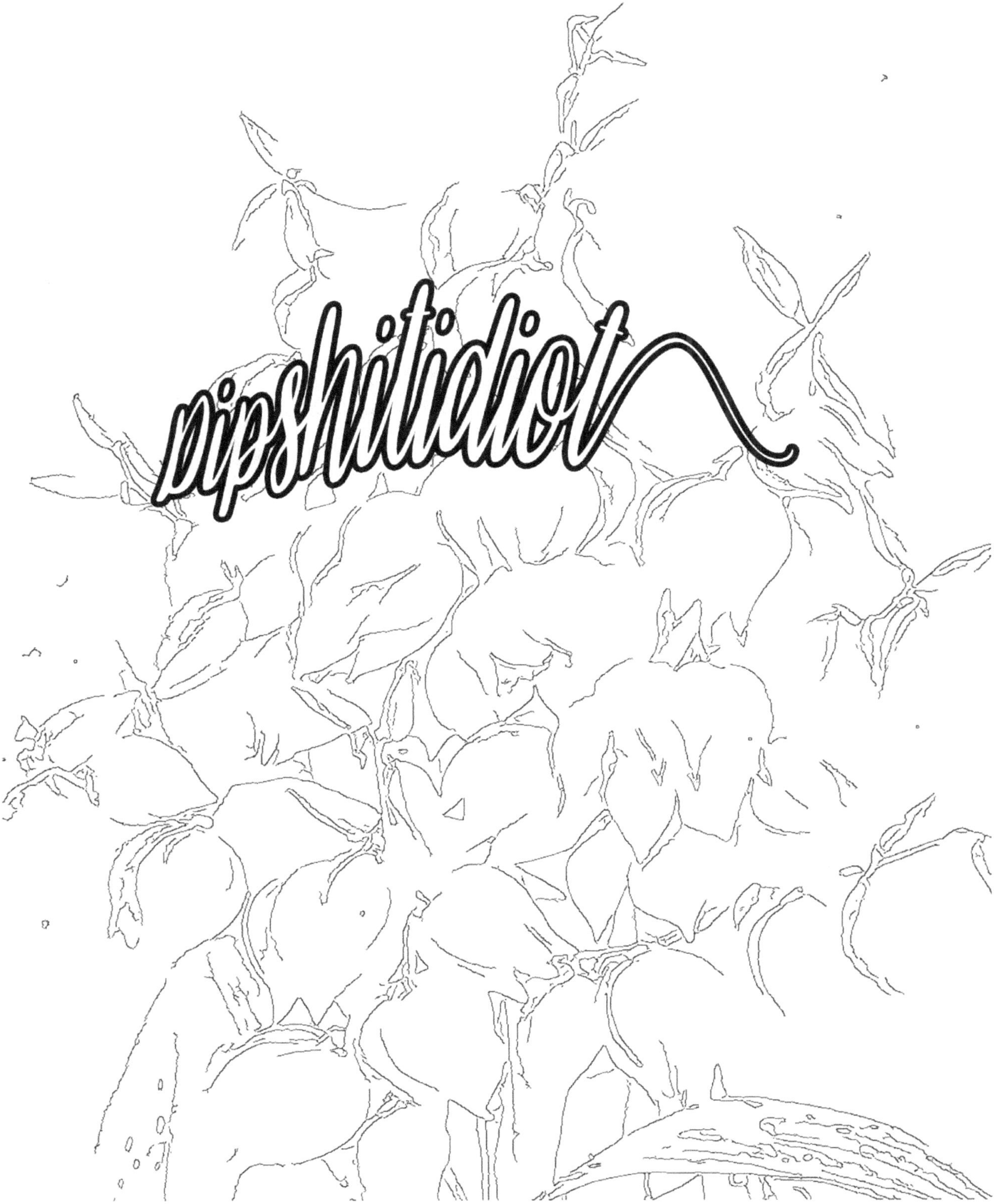
Dipshitidiot

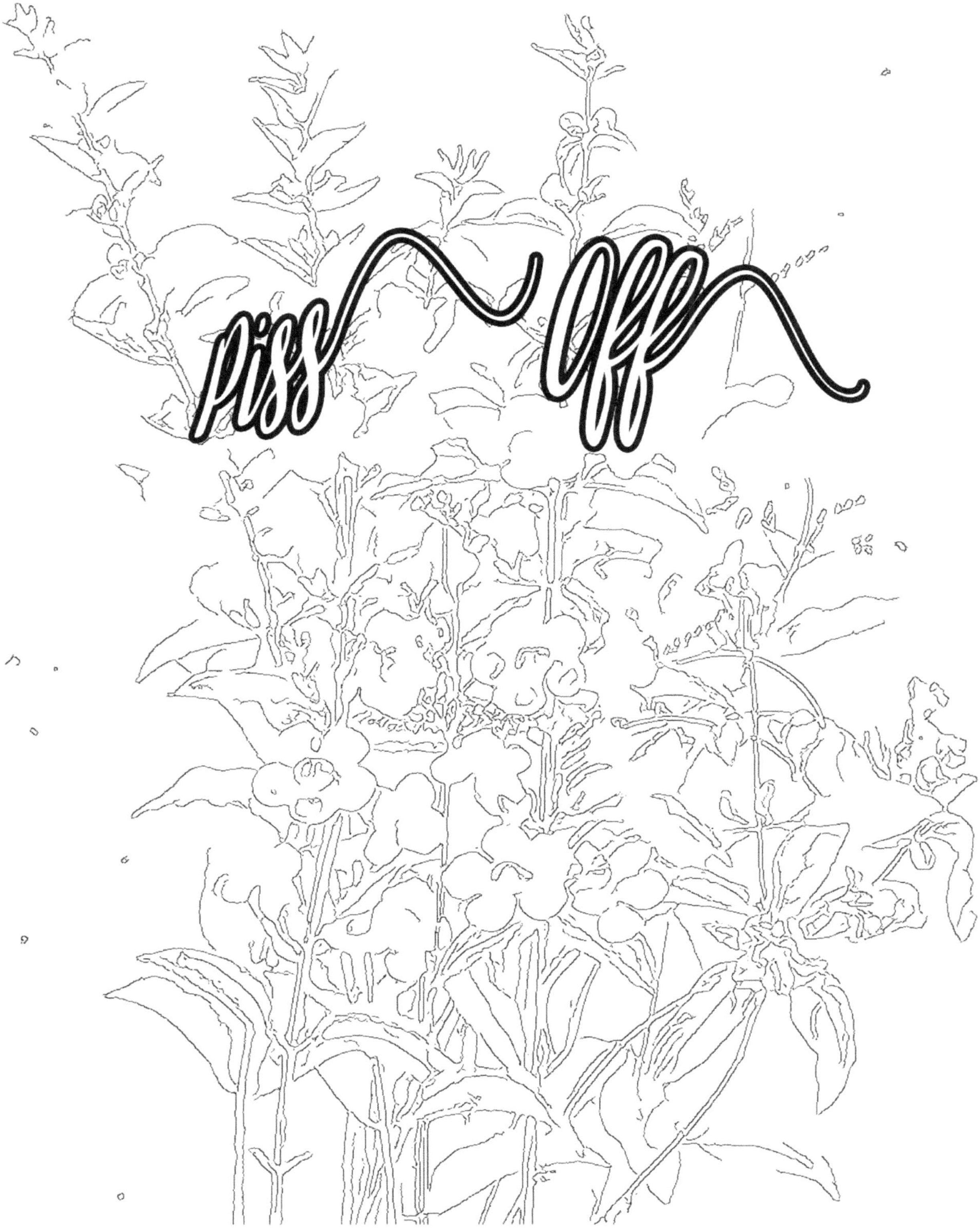
Piss Off

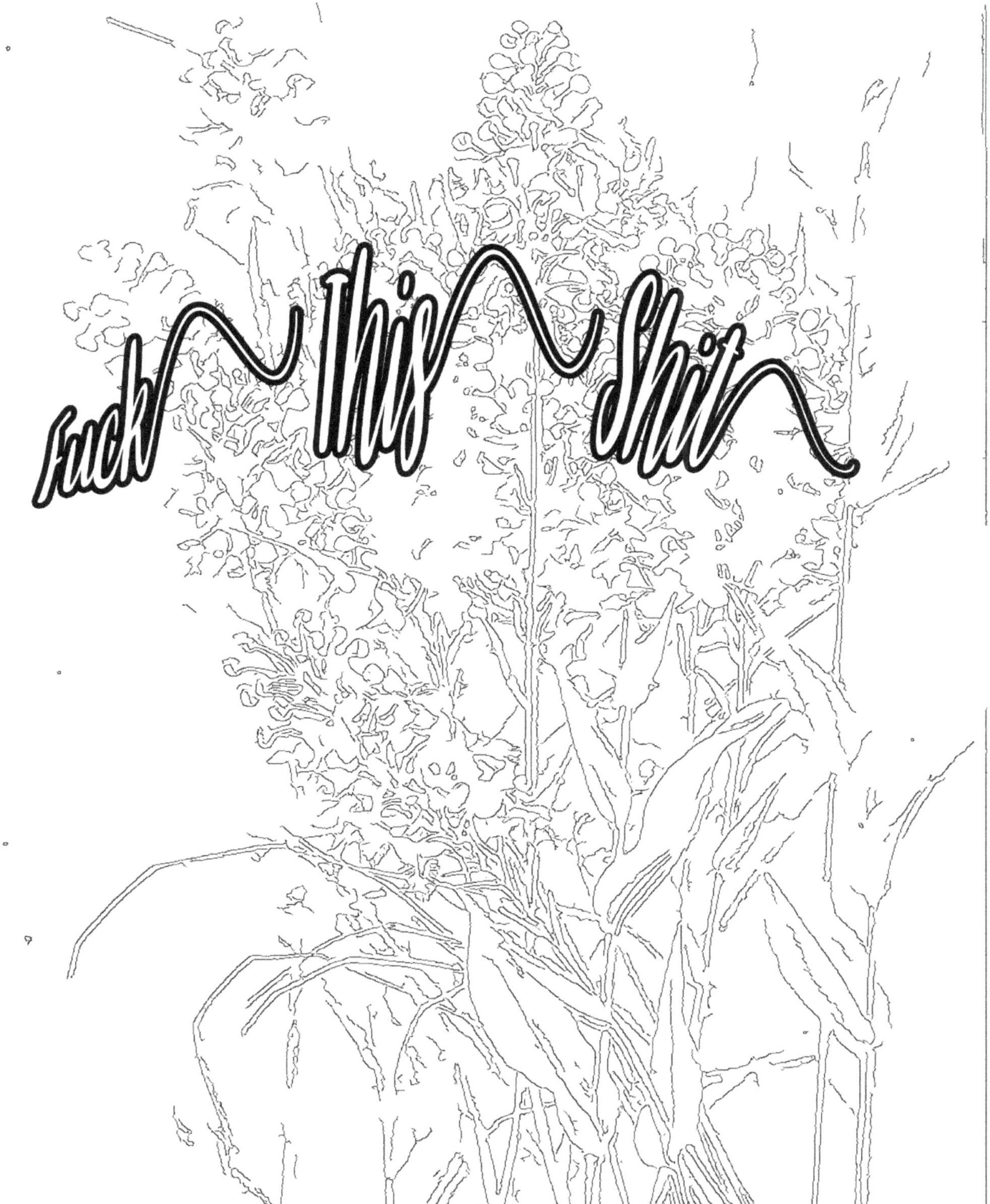
Fuck This Shit

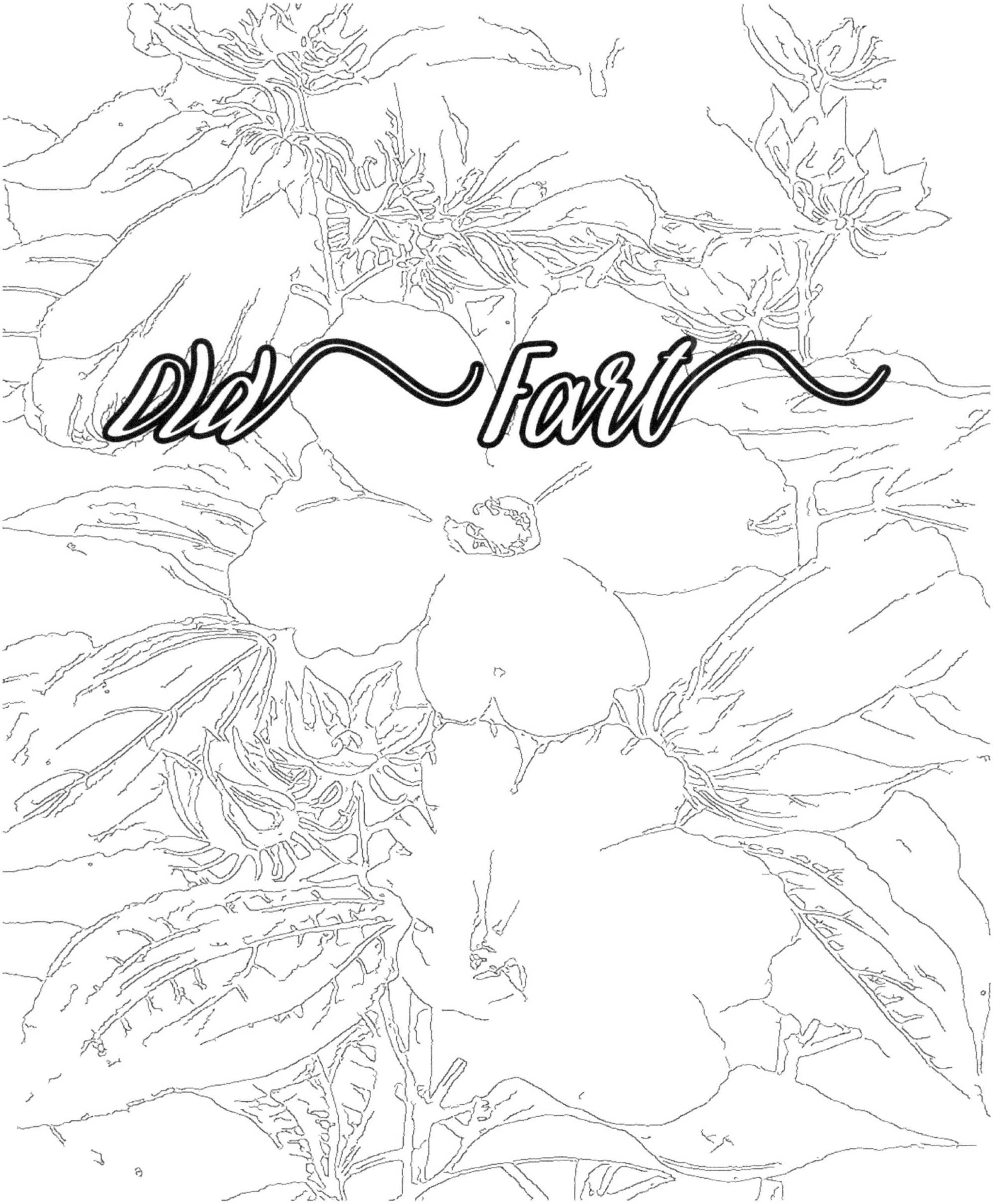
Old Fart

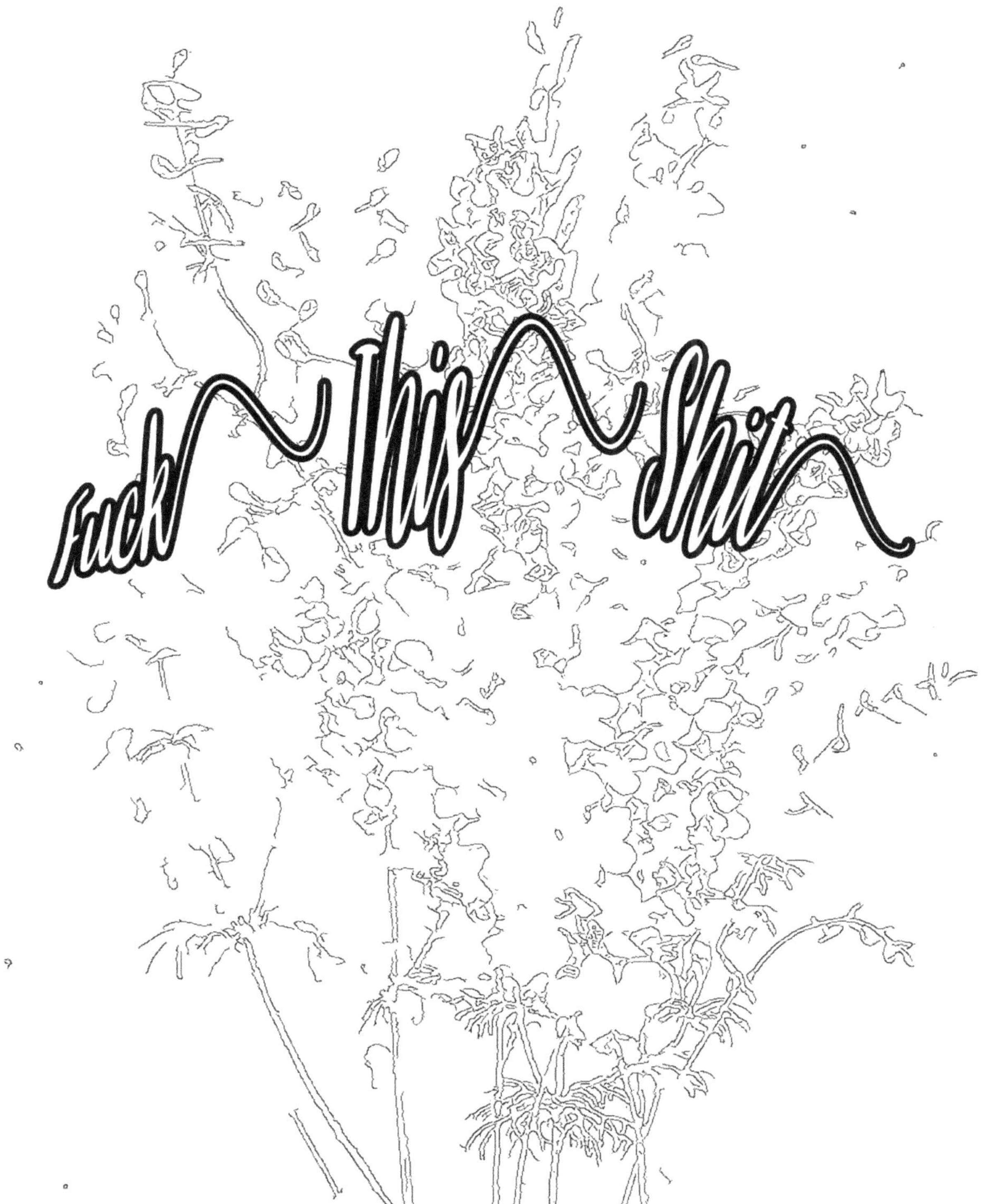
Fuck This Shit

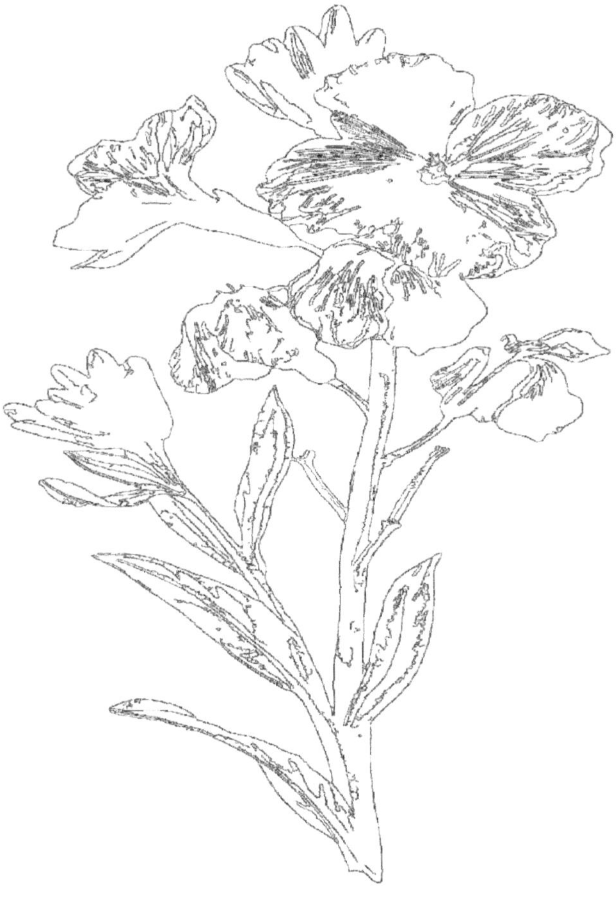

Have a good day.

www.ingramcontent.com/pod-product-compliance
Lightning Source LLC
Chambersburg PA
CBHW081620220526
45468CB00010B/2958
9781983409677